The Colors of Me Too

The Colors of Me Too

A COLLECTION OF POEMS

MAYA AND JELLO

Contents

Author's Note

So you've tasted of the honey in my first book of this series 'The Colors of Me' and now you've found yourself wanting more. Kudos to you.

There's no shame in it. You just know a good thing when you see it. Funny enough, I am hoping by now that there are millions of people just like you. Thank you from the bottom of my heart. When people like yourself read and enjoy my work, I feel like a chef who created something so masterfully delicious that people were left licking their fingers and craving more. So without further ado, allow me to take your hand and welcome you, to 'The Colors of Me Too.'

Read, enjoy, read again then share.

Acknowledgements

I would once again like to thank my son Denzel for the beautiful cover art. It is almost as beautiful as the colors of You.

To my family for all their love and support through out the years.

To my friend Viv who lends an ever willing ear to all the drama that is my life. God bless you.

And to all the colorful characters I have encountered so far in my life. Your energies, good or bad, have ignited the colors in me.

My Inspiration

*Lack of knowledge of self fuels genocide.
When we step into true self awareness, our
existence is less likely to be trivialized.*

Judah

You make records
Then you scratch them
Design clothes
Then you trash them
Got the whole world dancing to the beat
Cool to walk like you
Talk like you
Judah
Do you know who you are?
Can you feel all that is in you?
All that comes from you?
Judah
Do you know who you are?
You were stripped of your riches
Thrown in the gutter
Whipped, chained, hunted, lynched
Yet you rise up from the dust
And like your Father
Create life from the ashes around you
Rise up Judah and return
Return
Quiet the noise
The voices inside you
Planted by those who wish to blind you

Your prodigal children
Open your eyes and look around
Open your eyes
And put down the gun.

Maya and Jello
01/21/2019

My Inspiration

Picking up the pieces and moving on.

How Do You Forget

What do you do
When the only person who feels right
Seems to be all wrong?
What do you do when the only one you want to touch you
Seems miles and miles away?
What do you do
When the only voice that soothes your soul is silent?
What do you say to your heart as it cries?
What do you feed to your soul as it dies?
How do you calm the raging storms of desire?
How do you quiet?
How do you ease the pain of the loss?
How do you forget…
How do you forget…… to remember.

Maya and Jello
04/19/2017

My Inspiration

Self esteem is a hell of a thing.
Without it you are apt to settle for less.

On The DNL

What do you want with me Gigolo
I ain't no Ho
Just let me be.

Why you calling me Gigolo
I ain't no Ho
I set you free.

Why you texting me Gigolo
I ain't no Ho
Said I was your Bae for life
Still we're on the Down 'N' Low.

Got your ole lady at home
Yet you calling me on the phone
Making promises
That you just cannot keep.

Leave me alone gigolo
I ain't no Ho
All you want to do is Creep.

Got the whole world thinking
That we're in something
That we're together…
Still
You ain't never paid a bill.

Took what you could from my hand
Told everyone you're my man
Can't say the last time I saw you
I just can't understand.

Leave me alone Gigolo
I ain't no Ho
Just take a flying leap
If all you want to do
Is Creep.

Maya and Jello
03/08/2019

My Inspiration

Uncle Frankie and early Tap dancers.

UNCLE FRANKIE

Tah da-Dah-dap
Tah da-Dah-dap
Tah-da-Dah
Tah-da-Dah
Tah da-Dah-dap

Click-a-tik clic
Click-a-tik clic
Click-a-tik click-a-tik
Click-a-tik clic

Flattened soda caps
Under your shoe
Mr. Bojangles
Got nothing on you.

Maya and Jello
03/06/2019

My Inspiration

*So many times going through the motions is
used as a substitute for the real deal.*

The Morning After

She gazed. . . Awake
The walls her friend
Thoughts taken back
To yester-then
And longs her lover would awake
Her body in his arms to take.

They both know that it's dead somehow
But they keep it going on
'Cause when it's good it's better
But when it's not, it's bitter.

The love was hot
The passions wild
Yet in the midst
You know,
They both kept fantasizing
To keep the love aglow.

The morning comes
And sunlight kisses
Between their worn out bodies
No more as one
The passion's done
And life is what it used to be.

Maya and Jello
01/01/1988

My Inspiration

*Words are important. What we say can
build up or tear apart a relationship.*

HE SAID….SHE SAID

He said, I love your name
She said, I love yours too.

He said, I want this woman
And then handed her an apple.
She said, thank you.

He said, I'm not her husband
But I'm putting in my application.
She said, "you?"
"You wouldn't last 5 minutes."
They chuckled.

She said, I love you
He said….
He lied, "I'm off the market."
She said, "if every and any woman could do
Then
I'm just not the woman for you."

Maya and Jello
05/30/2015

LOVE
be with
observe
hold
listen
sense
respect
create
serve
care
welcome
accept
appreciate
allow
engage
thank
embrace
nurture
attend
let be
share
witness
trust
behold
connect
forgive
value
befriend
play
express
encourage
liberate

My Inspiration

You can't fall in love if you won't let go of your fears.

The Call Of Love

I remember how he held me.
How he kissed me..
And my soul bleeds.
Tell me you love me
And release my soul from this prison of uncertainty
Tell me you love me
And free my heart from the torture of rejection.

So many times we drifted apart
So many chances to say "no" to love
So much effort spent in denial
So much time spent suppressing the urges
So much energy wasted....
Fighting the flow...
Swimming against the current
Exhausted?
Now give up the fight
Love beckons you to take her hand
And taste of her wonders
Don't be afraid
Surrender to her
She's gentle and trusting
And sweet to the taste.

Maya and Jello
03/10/2008

What
should
I do?

*I know of so many people trapped in this situation.
Love should never be put in the balance with a
dollar bill. It makes for a miserable existence.*

Cheaper To Keep Her

They say it's cheaper to keep her
And who am I to disagree
The figures speak for themselves
But then, there is Eternity.

No Sleep
Can't keep
Your eyes off of tricks.

No romance
No finance
No peace
No release.

Nothing's bright
Save bursts of light
That spell S....O.....S
As you sink deeper and deeper
Into the same ole mess.

You look in the mirror
A face ten fifteen years older
You stare for a while
No joy.
No smile.

Surrounded yet alone
Tolerated, not celebrated
More invested
Less interested.

Alive
But not living
Decades lost to mere existence
You've given up a part of your soul.

You've gambled
The toys, the boys
The girls, the noise
To keep yourself so out of touch.

Then if it be true
That it's cheaper to keep her
Tell me why
Why my love
That it's costing you
So much.

Maya and Jello
02/16/2018

My Inspiration

Wrote this poem shortly before my mother passed.
In retrospect I think she telepathically wrote it.

Sleepless Nights

I don't want to leave it all behind
If you want me
'Cause I want you.
I don't want to give up on us
If you need me
'Cause I need you.
I don't want to say goodbye
If you'd be miserable
'Cause I'd be miserable too.
I don't want to throw it all away
If you love me
'Cause I love you.

Maya and Jello
11/16/2002

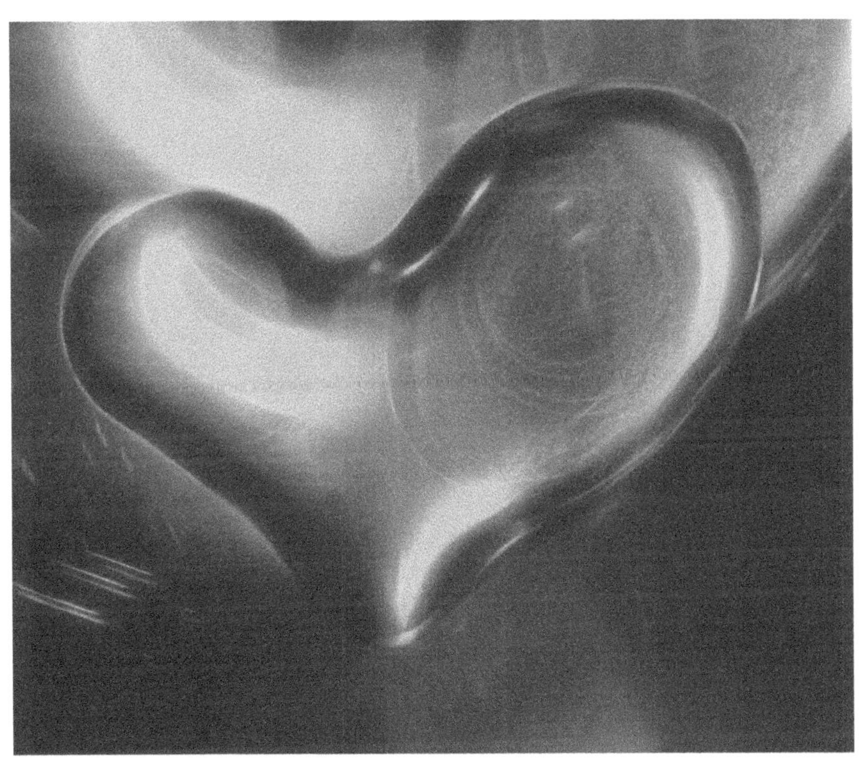

My Inspiration

It's the simple things in life.

BRING ME A GLASS OF WATER

Bring me a glass of water
That it may satisfy my thirst.

That I may drink
And feel its wetness
Trickle down my chest
And off my nipples
Down that sacred path
To quench my fires.

Bring me a glass of water
That my lips may taste you
And your waters
Could be mine.

Bring me a glass of water
With your heart in it
So as I drink
I can make it mine
Forever.

Maya and Jello
02/21/2017

My Inspiration

Haters will hate.
I was once told "The best revenge is living well".

TOUCHEZ

(Translated)

They'll laugh at you
And play the game
You know they're all the same
Pretentious, devious, cold backstabbers
Yet you're the one they'll blame.

They'll ride you, if you'd let them
From one place to the next
And when you tell them how they're bad
They'll get so blasted vexed.

They call you crazy
You're a drama queen
Your facts aren't right
You always change the scene.

But one day this will pass away
And you will stand alone
Triumphant
'Cause you lived your life
For the One who's on the throne.

So stand up tall
Stand up straight
Hold fast and be strong.

'Cause in the end
As time will tell
They are the ones who are wrong.

Maya and Jello
09/13/2010

My Inspiration

To whom much is given much is required.
Tread lightly.

The Fall Of Pharaoh

A leader chosen by God he was
But Pharaoh had a vice.
Much power he possessed to rule
But this demon ruled his life.

Fair maidens in the land he saw
As treasures to be sought.
And one by one, like conquered lands
To lay with him he brought.

No thought as to how he hurt their life
No thought as to how he brought them strife
No thought as to what became of them
As long as his bidding was done.

A chosen one, a man God sought
But in closed chambers Pharaoh thought.
Oh Egypt land,
I am the king of love and wine and merriment.
I have no one to answer to
And all your wives shall have unbent.

But one day as he stood to rule.
So strong, so proud and debonair
The people by the thousands came
Their fearless leader now to hear.

But none could have conceived his fate.

A harlot from the town stood up
And with her sultry voice she said
Oh Pharaoh, you forgot your smock
When last night we did lay in bed.

A HUSH descended on the crowd
The hearts that bled
The hopes that crushed
Their fearless leader now reduced
Not just mere man
But worse…
A Slut!

Maya and Jello
01/01/2003.

My Inspiration

Rejuvenating balance of quiet reflection.

Quiet Moments

Sometimes Life is about quiet moments.
Lounging on a bed in a moonlit room
Moon-shine through the window
Reminiscing of childhood comforts
Carefree thoughts
Braiding your hair
Just because.

Maya and Jello
02/2009

My Inspiration

The importance of young men and women guarding their virtue.

First Time

Who are you?

A man you say

And I?

A woman

We exist

Or do we really?

We meet

And nature takes her course

At that moment

Our hearts are all for the taking

But my soul feels the urgency

To resist.

Maybe. . . I say

I think to myself

I'll save my heart

When in return

I too can have yours

Time after time

I reached forth my hand

Only to return with empty arms and shattered dreams

But my soul felt the urgency

To Hope.

Separation
I tried to hide in hope
That my heart would learn a way of its own
Alone
But my soul felt the urgency
To be loved.

So there you were
And yet were not
Then so were we
Yet we were not
But my soul felt the urgency
To share.

We met
And nature took its course
I reached forth my hand
And there was your heart
In exchange for mine
But something was wrong.

The chill. . .. like stone
No blood. No feeling. . ..
No love
Your heart was

And yet was not
So then my soul felt the urgency
The urgency
To die.

Maya and Jello
01/01/1989

———❦———

WINNER

My Inspiration

Revelation 12:11

Victories

Boxed in by a cloud of thoughts
Wondering if I have anything to do with anything
Inexplicable, incalculable formulas
Trying to maybe trace events
Trying to maybe find the key
Trying to figure out how
So I asked
And the Spirit of God said
You don't need to know 'how'
You just need to know …
HOW
By the blood of the Lamb
And the Word of their testimony.

Maya and Jello
04/30/2017

TRINIDAD & TOBAGO
Home of
THE STEELPAN
TO EXIT

My Inspiration

*The first steel drum was invented just after World War 2
in Trinidad West Indies by one Winston 'Spree' Simon.*

Pan Love

The pan yard's
Where it all started
My love for it never departed
I don't give it the attention it needs
It's like it's growing weeds.

I truly love the sound it makes
And the hard work it takes
It's not easy like some cakes.

The flag I rep
I keep them on my set
Trini flags cover the pans
Could be on a Carnival caravan.

Making tunes off the top
It just hits me like a raindrop
It's like working with another –
Like co-op.

The pans covered in silver
I ain't talking surfer
It's like a wish come true
Don't call me Timmy Turner 2.

The love for my pans won't fade
I might of took a while and swayed
But I'm here to stay
And soar like a Blue Jay.

With the pans
Is where I belong
And there is where
I make my song.

Denzel Honore
2018

My Inspiration

A workaholic may just be someone trying to escape inner turmoil.

Water Works

When I think about you
And the passions arise
It doesn't take long
For tears to fall from my eyes.

Restless nights
I crave your touch
I wish it didn't
Hurt so much.

My days are haunted
With memories
Of tender moments
Those lend no ease.

There's a constant calling
From the depth of my soul
Return my love
And make me whole.

Occupying myself from day to day
Each moment filled
No time to play.

But when I think about you
And the passions arise
It doesn't take long
For tears to fall from my eyes.

Maya and Jello
11/15/2018

My Inspiration

*Trip to the lovely island of Okinawa for a Global
Health Conference. Wonderful people.
Miss you guys.*

Okinawa

Okinawa was a dream
No
A fantasy
Come true.

Since then
We seemed
To have drifted
Apart
Yet
I'm still
So
In love
With
You.

Maya and Jello
09/15/2013

My Inspiration

We cannot move forward carrying the weight of the past around.

THE EXORCISM

Sometimes I feel like I want to be...
Locked in a bear hug embrace with you.
I want you to hug me
'Til all the hurt's squeezed out of me.
I want to cry
Cry and cry and cry
'Til the tears wash over your shoulders
And the snot and drool
Make your shirt stick to your chest.
I want to scream
'Til you feel my pain.
'Til I lay breathless,
And limp, in your arms.
Void of all that's past
And ready...
to love again.

Maya and Jello
07/16/2011

My Inspiration

Maybe raindrops are meant to hit our heads not umbrellas.

RAINDROPS

Let the rain of Heaven
Fall
Like raindrops from the sky.

Let me feel the gentle
Washing of your Grace
Let me feel the cleansing
Of every drop of Mercy
As it hits my head
And washes me.

Let me feel the cleansing
Of all that is obstructive and evil
The gentle washing away.

Let me feel the blessing
Carried in each drop
As commissioned and purposed
They anoint me with their special blessings.

Let the rain of Heaven
Fall
And renew
And build anew
And give life.

Let me smell the sweet after fragrance
And bask in the coolness
Of the after glow.

Let the rains of Heaven
Fall.

Maya and Jello
12/06/2015

My Inspiration

Is it possible to love too much?
Someone once said "if you love something, set it free."

Sweet Mother

You carried me for nine months
You brought me into this world
I dwelt within your bosom
Protected from the cold.

You taught me what was right from wrong
As I grew from day to day.
You showed me how to stand alone
To walk, to share, to play.

My every step your eyes surveyed,
Your thoughts were mine, desires too.
Each day was made of lessons filled
With what to say and what to do.

So I became the reality,
Of the dream you always dreamt.
And closed up in my little own world
Never really knew what life meant.

Many years have passed, I'm older now
But your attitude has not changed.
You still keep me chained to your bosom
And to the outside world estranged.

It's true that I'm your only son
But you must realize
I've got a life like you to live
I've got to get myself a wife.

You said you understand my plight
But other things are more important.
God knows just how I try to fight
Yet you insist on having what you want.

I still depend on you somewhat
So I guess I should be humble
Forget about sharing…loving…life
And all that mumble-jumble.

The time has flown SWEET MOTHER DEAR
You've gone and left me alone
Despite the fame and fortune I've got
There's no friend to call on the phone.
I've learned to reach the heights in life
You've got to get right up and go.
But this cancerous solitude and emptiness mother
To you my dear……I owe.

Maya and Jello
11/02/1986

My Inspiration

*Sitting down doing homework with my little
boy. I remember how he would look at
a math problem and arrive at the answer in
his head, while I insisted over and
over again that he had to show the steps on paper.
When God shows up
He negates the process and shows up with the answer.*

Miracles

Purpose.....Preparation.......and Pain
The Process
Only God can override.
We call them
Miracles.

Maya and Jello
09/25/2015

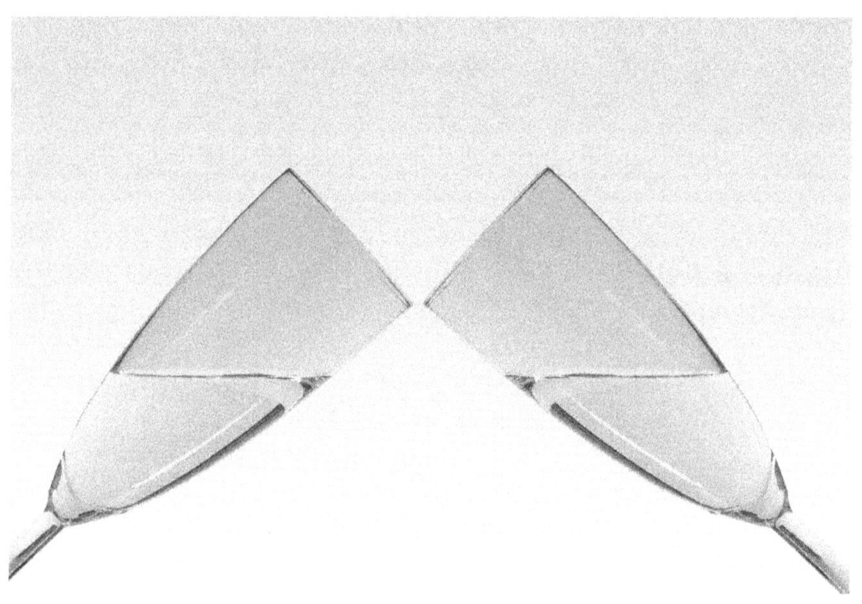

My Inspiration

Fun with Alkaline water.

The Gift

It's our Anniversary she said
I pretended to know.

Maybe I'll buy a present later
At the Mall
They'll know what'll please her.

Started my day
Wolfed down some coffee
Dropped the kids off
Paid all the school fees.

Stuck in traffic
Late for work
Boss announced
We're going broke.

Worked through lunch
Didn't get to the mall
Got to drop off the kids
Girl to ballet
Boy to football.

Dinner time
And I came up empty
It's our Anniversary
I pretended to know.

Couldn't buy the present later
Had to think
Just couldn't hurt her.

So off to the kitchen
To my SD501
It's all the present that she needs
My searching now was done.

Gift wrapped
Tiny spray bottle filled with 4.5
Glass bottle full of 9.0
A dark container of 11.5
And a spray bottle filled with 2.4.

Then I wrote a note that said...

I can't believe we've come this far
This gift represents
All that's deep and real
In my heart.

9.0 to keep us on the go
11.5 no gook can survive
2.4 to keep us clean
And more
The 4.5 to keep the beauty alive.

She looked at me
Then raised her glass
And said
This love for sure will last.

Maya and Jello
01/2015

My Inspiration

Getting back in the game.
The game of love, that is.

Have You Ever?

Have you ever felt a bursting, uncontrollable desire
To be held by that special someone?
Just to feel their embrace
To smell their essence
To taste their kiss
Just to hear them groan with desire for you.
Have you ever been awake at night
Longing to be touched by that special someone?
Longing to see their smile
Longing to hear them laugh
Longing to look in to their eyes
Dying to share the passion you've caged up inside
Have you ever felt
Like feeling again?

Maya and Jello
06/01/2006

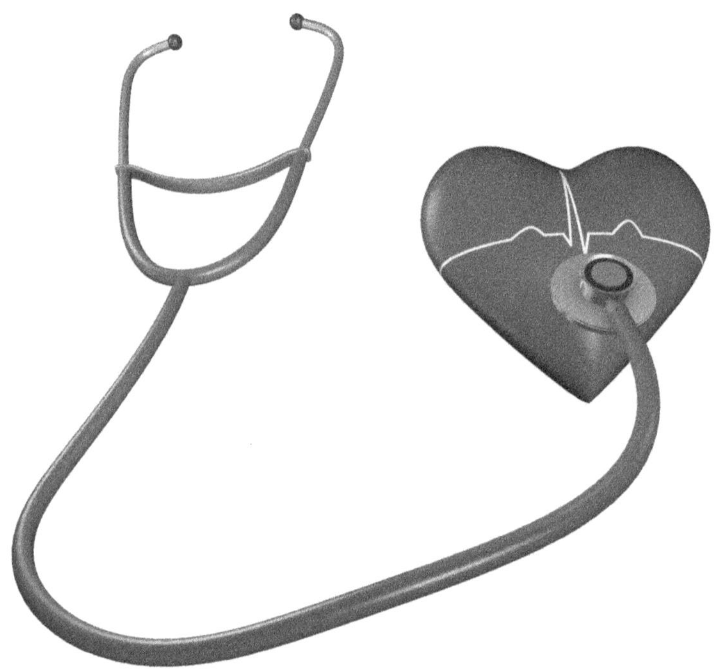

My Inspiration

*Some people bring with them a healing balm, a genuine
concern for the well being of others.
We call them Doctors.*

The Pill

So I called my Doctor
And had to ask him
"Doc, what did you do to me?"
"I still feel so groggy,"
What exactly do you mean my dear?
Well
I remember feeling hot all over
Then this feeling of sweet surrender
Came over my being.
It was as though my spirit had left my body
To a higher plane of sheer bliss
As my body lay weak and helpless,
Helpless to the force that had somehow captured my soul
The image in my head
Of my soul repeatedly traveling to the top of a mountain
Then down again
Kissing its tip
Oh so gently
Up and down…
Up and down …
Higher….higher…higher
Each time yearning to stay a little longer on the summit
Any way Doc, I still feel so relaxed
Oh so sleepy.
"Don't worry my dear", he replied
"You'll be fine
I just gave you something to take the edge off your pain."

Thank you I whispered
Thank you for caring
I smiled
Filled with anticipation of my next visit.

Maya and Jello
05/25/2002

My Inspiration

Raising two kids in the same environment does not guarantee they will have the same personal values.

Something to keep in mind when you are tempted to ask "Do you have a sister?"
Or "Do you have a brother?"

Sexy And Slutty

Sexy and Slutty
Were two little girls
Who lived in their Mom's house
For Free.
They did all the prepping
And maintained themselves
And often were asked out to tea.
Sexy was good
But Slutty was bad
They each had a hefty 'badonga'
But Sexy got all of the boys' hearts aglow
While Slutty was left there
To wonder.

Maya and Jello
04/08/2016

My Inspiration

Beautiful things happen when we give it all up to God.

The Prayer

Oh Lord, I feel a change coming on.

But I will not go, save You go with me.

I will not follow, save You lead.

I will not bend my back to toil

Save Your feet I can anoint and kiss.

I will not turn

Save Your face I can see.

Oh Holy God, I feel a change coming on

But if it is that I should stand still

If Your will be that I not move

Give me the grace.

I lay my wants, my needs at the foot of Your cross

'Cause I know if I follow and You don't lead

I'd be lost.

If I toil and not worship at Your feet

I toil in vain.

If I rise and stand not on the Rock that is Christ

My fall is sure.

Oh Merciful and Everlasting Father
Hear my cry.
Turn not Your ear from me.
Encapsulate me in Your love and mercy
And let Your Divine will saturate… SATURATE
S… A… T… U… R… A… T… E
EVERY aspect of my life.

Maya and Jello
12/28/2002

My Inspiration

Forgiveness is a healing force.

Sweet Release

I've waited all these years just to hear you
apologize to me like a real friend
Just to feel the release
As you pull the dagger out of my chest,
As you break the walls down with sincerity.
Just to celebrate as the walls come down.
It was our openness that connected us..
Or so I thought
Yet your secrets and deceptions separated us
Come on.
I've waited all this time to hear you ask me.
I've waited all this time...and I'm still waiting... hoping
Hoping that you would give me the chance to reply
"I forgive you."

Maya and Jello
04/09/2008

My Inspiration

There is much to say about promiscuity and protection.
Remembering that every action has an equal and opposite reaction.

Jamaica Vacation

The island breeze is beautiful
The ocean's inviting too.
The women fall over easy
But there's one thing I want you to do
Keep dat ting in yuh pants baby
Strap dat ting up I'm warning you
Cause AiDS don't know you know me
And I want to keep knowing you.

Maya and Jello
08/13/2002

My Inspiration

Angels come in many forms.
So do good friends.

My Raven

It is true that this life is not designed for lasting pleasures
If it were
We'd never dream of Heaven
If it were
We'd seldom call on God.

But I believe that there are those blessings
Provisions in our deserts
Sheer miracles
Forever precious.

I know not whether you were my cloud by day
Cool shade from the scorching of the desert sun
Or the pillar of fire to guide my way
Through the darkest of nights
Or the rock that spewed forth water
So I didn't die of thirst
Or that Raven that brought me manna
So I had the strength, in spite of it all
To continue putting one foot in front of the other.

But I do believe these were provisions
Granted by the Great Provider.

Could it then be
That we're not supposed to fall in love
With the bearers of such blessings?
Are we then called
To give all adoration
To the Great Provider?

You my love, were my Raven
Bringing manna,
Restoring Sanity,
Giving strength.

Each day I looked forward
To eating from your hands
Sharing, caring moments.
Each day I set my eyes to the skies
In search of you
To hear you call.

I craved you.
I craved what you brought.
I craved the glimpses of Canaan
I saw in your eyes.

God forgive me
For falling so deeply in love with you.
You were simply
The bearer of my blessing
My rock….. My fire…. My cloud
My Raven.

Maya and Jello
03/26/2016

My Inspiration

Hard-headed people are exhausting.

Deja Vu

I once knew a man
A man like you
Couldn't tell him what to say
Couldn't tell him what to do.

Wrong as rain
Yet
Couldn't refrain
From talking a whole lot of smack.

Now all alone
There's no one at home
Bet he'd pay anything
To get his life back.

Blaming everyone he knew
For the things he shouldn't do.

I once knew a man
A man like you.

Maya and jello
03/16/2019

My Inspiration

Fetching water. Oftentimes the Water Authority in Trinidad and other areas of the Caribbean would shut off the water supply without warning.

DE STAN PIPE

Weh de wahtah
De wahtah goahn
Dehy tun afh de wahtah?
Yea de wahtah goahn
When de wahtah cohmen bac?
We duh noh
How we guh do de laundry,
Ahn bade, ahn brush we teet, ahn cook?
Luhk bohys
Take two bukits each
Go to de stan pipe up de street
Fill up de bahrils bahk in de yahrd
Only ah haf mile up de rohd
Dat eh so hard
Form ah wahta brigade
Bohys bring de wahta
Girhls fill up de bahrils
Mind yuh speed
Dat buckit haf empty
Good
Keep it cohmin
We goh haf wahta feh de nex
Two days.

Maya and Jello
03/16/2019

Sometimes we know where we belong.
What feels right.
But we are not willing to make the sacrifice to get it.

Africa

You shoke my hand
And I felt your wanting
Pulling me in
Inviting me to make sweet love to you.

Don't you understand?
You are my bashert
My heart.
My lord, we reigned in times past
Or don't you remember?

You beckon me
But I cannot answer
Cause the place you have in your life
Does not befit a Queen.

I see the longing in your eyes
And yearn to give in.
But the throne at my side
Requires a King.

Make haste my love
For I am waiting 'til the day
You return home.

'Til then I pray
That on that day
My arms still need to embrace you
My lips still yearn to kiss yours.
I pray the fire in my loins
Burns just as hot with desire for you
And on that day
You find in me
What completes you.

Maya and Jello
06/07/2014

My Inspiration

*The transformation that takes place in
your life when Love arrives.*

The Power Of Love

As the painful years go by
You fall into this rut
"I'm too old and set in my ways
No need to get to know anyone else
Or have anyone get to know me"
But then something strange happens.
While you're hiding your true self from the world
You meet someone
Someone who reaches inside,
Inside the cocoon you woven for yourself
They touch you,
And you become alive again.
Only this time....
You're beautiful,
You've sprouted wings,
And now.... you can fly.

The ugly caterpillar days are no more
And life is new, adventurous
And all there **is, is Beauty, New beginnings and Hope**
You've fallen in love...
And Love has worked that ole black magic on you.

Maya and Jello
05/13/2005

*Sometimes we become so preoccupied with how
we are seen by others.
To heck with it!
What does God see?*

Father's Vision

As I laid in my bed
In a pensive mood
Drowning in my own thoughts
Of purpose and existence.
My mind paralyzed
By a cocktail of questions
I asked.
"Tell me Father.
What do You see?"
"What do **You** see
When you look at me?"
And without hesitation He answered
"A Poem"
"A beautiful writing."
"A work of Art."

Maya and Jello
02/16/2018

What are people saying:

'A great poet can in seconds teleport you into a different world. Minutes later they'll bring you back questioning the reality of your very existence and the world around you. Maya and Jello is such a poet. '   Rev. Dr. Patricia Sealy

Make sure to get your copy of 'The Colors of Me.' Available in audio-book format.
'A beautifully read well narrated and incredibly written book of poetry...'
Author/Reviewer Anthony Avina